T0067223

For All You Know:

Possible Reasons You May Still Be Unhappy On The Path To Enlightenment

TERAL EVELYN CHAMPION

Foreword by Rev. Dr. Peter Fabian, D.Mn.

BALBOA.
PRESS

A DIVISION OF HAY HOUSE

Balboa Press books may be ordered through booksellers or by contacting:

Balboa Press
A Division of Hay House
1663 Liberty Drive
Bloomington, IN 47403
www.balboapress.com
1 (877) 407-4847

Print information available on the last page.

ISBN: 978-1-5043-3046-6 (sc)
ISBN: 978-1-5043-3047-3 (e)

Balboa Press rev. date: 10/25/2015

Dedication

This book is dedicated to Nujemi, my daughter. I never thought being a single parent came with so many benefits; the lessons, the laughter and the love…you made it something wonderful.

Many thanks to Karen Rose, Bev, Judy and Sally. Your patience, encouragement and guidance kept me moving forward.

To my guru, Amma, who guides me inward with her unending embraces. And to the late Maharishi Mahesh Yogi for the incredible experience of transcendence.

Contents

Foreword

This is not an easy read.
It was not intended to be.

If what you are used to in your spiritual journey is reading uplifting and full of goodness and light, while some of this is there in this book that is not the purpose.

Teral takes us on a journey of blood and guts—the hard times so many of us face in life. In other words, reality.

It is a real life and it is her life. With all the difficulties of being a single mom, sometimes homeless, at times an alcoholic, she never gives up the quest for inner peace and inner truth.

You can never afford a negative thought because, as Teral illustrates in these writings, there are consequences which we might not be aware of. In the words of Edgar Cayce, "mind is the builder" and we learn how pain can be perpetuated by our thoughts and expressions of anger, resentment and jealousy.

What is different about her message from some other writings is that Teral thought she was doing all the right things to achieve enlightenment. She did all the standard enlightenment practices from having gurus, to learning meditation, to practicing enlightenment techniques daily for many decades. Teral eventually learns that techniques alone were not going to bring the peace she longed for.

Come take this journey with Teral and see if there may be an insight or two into your own life's pattern that could be made different by the simple message she shares with us.

-Rev. Dr. Peter Fabian, D.Mn.,
minister in the United Church of Christ,
and professor of psychology at Edgewood
College, Madison, Wisconsin

Acknowledgements

Many thanks to the writing assistance program of the South Central Library of Madison, Wisconsin. Thanks also to Brian Knight and Zach Marshall for helping me edit this book.

The Purpose of This Book

This book is written for those of you who question your faith and your understanding of God. It's for those who have doubts about their spiritual practices. If you question yourself, your worth and how your life is unfolding, read on. I wrote it in an effort to help bring some clarity of thought. And to offer some understanding you may not have developed while studying all those spiritual tools you keep on your shelf. Hopefully reading this book will shed some light on why you are still unhappy on your path towards the light.

Writing this manual is my effort to reach out to those who suffer. As I watched online spiritual programs about enlightenment, I saw two individuals crying; they seemed desperate. They spoke of the unhappiness in their lives. While each person was on a separate show, their concerns were the same. On a T.V. program, a letter was read by the host. It was previously written by someone experiencing suicidal thoughts. All of these individuals spoke about problems that were very similar to mine: "What is wrong with my life and why can't I do anything to fix it." I felt their pain; as they cried, I cried. This book is my response to them and thousands of others like them.

Another goal of this book is to neutralize the energy on the path's playing field, so to speak. Those of us on this journey are sometimes met with other travelers who are further along than us, so it would appear. They are well-versed on the topic of enlightenment and have a calm demeanor. We approach them with our concerns because they seem to have what we want. In short, it would be great if we could get our questions addressed by them without getting our heads chewed off. I need to say, not everyone has responded to my problems like some kind of consciousness police. Some individuals with whom I have shared my concerns have directed me in a gentle way and for them I am grateful.

The idea to write this book was motivated by a relief from depression. What brought on this mood was unpleasant memories that just kept playing out in my mind. I had recalled experiences with many people whom I met at workshops over the years or from close relationships. Some individuals from these groups would shout and point at me aggressively. The energy projected from them was ill fitting. It felt as if their comments, didn't apply to me which left me feeling so misunderstood and isolated. Though I chose to walk a spiritual path, I somehow felt trapped as I felt confused and nowhere else to turn.

We have all heard the term "get it." In this book the two words are synonymous with having a spiritual awakening. I trust you know this already. I also understand what you read in this book may be nothing new to you. For me, I read everything I could about how to advance spiritually and still couldn't grasp the core of the message in front of me. So many have tried to tell me the truth, the way out of my madness, but I wouldn't listen. This is because I thought I already knew what they had to say. Because I turned a deaf ear, I could not see how messed up I was. Therefore, with the use of my personal journey, I am writing this book as a way to assist you in your awakening process.

"Our thoughts about our experiences in any given moment, is what causes us to either suffer or to feel joy."

Introduction

I never expected to live my life in total chaos, one of poverty and homelessness. As a spiritual seeker, I thought I would be living in a beautiful home on easy street. Little did I know, the road to la-la land was blocked by an energy that would take a daily practice to remove. Who knew changing your mind constantly would lead to inner peace?

Various leaders who hosted movies and documentaries on spiritual growth had houses, cars and friendships with many people. They appeared happy and somewhat awakened. So as I watched these references, I thought I would someday acquire these things which I felt necessary to simply live my life.

After all, I followed the steps to success; I got an education and earned a master's degree. I also followed the most golden rule of them all: "Do unto others..." But still, something was completely lacking for me.

It took thirty plus years of meditation practices before I realized I was missing the reason for starting a spiritual journey in the first place. You make life what you want it to be. When it doesn't unfold in the way you plan, it's time to take notice and make some changes.

As a single mother, I read as many self-help books as I could get my hands on. I also watched programs on how to live a more fulfilling life without misery. I passed what I learned down to my daughter as I spoke in words she could understand. When she was nine, for example, she began to manifest what she wanted and her first efforts handed her a trip to Disney Land with her friends, all expenses paid.

While my daughter says she had a decent childhood, mine wasn't the best, but it did keep me in line. I grew up with my grandparents and back then, elders in my family did not hesitate to whip you whenever they even suspected you misbehaved. And if you really did act a fool, you got a more aggressive punishment. It wasn't uncommon to go to school with welts and bruises on my body. And if that wasn't enough, my grandfather would make frequent visits down the hall to my room. His footsteps on the old squeaky floor would announce his need not long before his scraggly beard touched my face. As traumatic as those events were, I have managed to get through life in spite of it all. But I would not change a thing; it made me who I am today: someone who respects others and wants to make a positive impact on people's lives.

I'm a social worker who strives to help save the world in my own small way. My long term plan was to open a private practice and do what I was trained to do, counseling. After all my arduous efforts to make my dreams come true, nothing became of them. Now, they seem like echoes in a past so distant that the idea doesn't even feel like a part of me anymore.

It's one thing for someone else to get in the way of what you want; you can either tell them where to go in no uncertain terms or simply push them aside -- just kidding. But for you to be the reason why you failed, well, that's a whole new animal you're dealing with.

While reading this text, you will notice the pronouns will change throughout the book; they change from first to second or third person unexpectedly. This is done to enhance the flow of ideas or points being made. At times these pages may read as a stern voice. You may get angry from reading this book and want to throw it across the room. It might scare you to know that you are not perfect or that you really don't understand enough about how to become happy. As my mother used to say, "The truth hurts." Sometimes, it's scary for that reason. You can be brave though, and bite the bullet and still live. Give yourself a chance and live your life without misery. It's your time now, to shine. Ah-ha moments are not just for some, they are also for you.

Though the message here may at times seem abrasive, at other times, I hope you can feel my sincere efforts to empathize with you, to show my understanding of what you are going through. I know you have been to hell on a one-way street. I want you to know I am with you and my plan here is to help you get back from that horrible existence. It's not a piece of cake, the road back, but for sure it's doable. Hey, if you have looked the devil in its mouth, the worse is over so smile, you are not alone. I hope you will continue to read this book. It's about my life in a nutshell, plus or minus a few scenarios. It explains why I continued to struggle no matter how many good deeds I performed or how much I practiced spirituality. May you extract from it what you need to continue to move forward on your path towards enlightenment.

But I tell you, you have to really want to get it, to feel better, to live a life without suffering. You have to want it like you wanted to see God on those dark nights when you felt like putting a knife to your wrist or swallowing a handful of assorted pills. You have to really let go of old bad habits you don't think you have and pay attention to those who tell you, you do. You can't have your ah-ha moment if you're not listening. And you certainly cannot have it if you give up, so press on; it could be in the next moment for all you know.

Chapter I

If You've Got It and You Know It

"When those around us are suffering, we can use our words to comfort them, instead of causing them more pain and suffering."

There are a few of you who have some amount of an awakening and feel the need to help others get it. I hope you understand I mean no ill will here. It is not my intentions to cause you any hard feelings or to blame you for the unhappiness of others. I only want to enlighten you to what may be going on for those who have not yet awakened. My intent is to inform you of how you are being received as you offer your expertise on what or how a seeker should think or behave on the path towards enlightenment. There are some travelers who are stuck, and because you present yourself with confidence and inner peace, they ask for your help. They express their concerns to you in hopes of getting some things figured out. Instead, they feel worse after confiding in you. I know it's not your fault that those of us who admit we are clueless feel attacked.

But it is not OK to yell at seekers who come to you for help; "It's always someone else's fault, you're the one…!" I've been told this all too often. But if one's consciousness is not on the appropriate level to understand a concept, all your well-meaning intentions to wake someone up is a waste of your breath. It feels emotionally abusive to the one you think you are helping when you raise your voice in anger. Again, I know you mean well as you give them your advice.

Try some compassion and patience or just leave us alone. We can feel bad all by ourselves without being yelled at. When we are being talked to in this manner, we quickly forget you are just trying to point the way out of our predicament. No one will get it until it is time for them to get it. Until that happens, we don't have a clue as to what you are trying to shove down our throats.

Seekers in this situation so badly want to enjoy life and experience an awakening. We have obsessed about it, and we prayed about it. We have done everything we know to make it happen. At some point, we feel frustrated, exhausted, confused, desperate and anxious. And the sense of hopelessness and deception feels like the tipping point, and we want to give up. We often just feel stupid, so give us a break, please.

Understand that one's level of consciousness determines their ability to process information. When a person lacks the level needed to understand a concept, no amount of head-jamming (banging their head against a wall) will make your point clear to them. It takes time, patience, love and compassion with such a person. If you are not capable of operating from a space in your heart, it's OK. But if you continue speaking with an aggressive tone, you may be causing some emotional damage to the individual you are trying to awaken, possibly driving them to want to commit suicide. We can use our words to lighten the load of others or to cause them pain and suffering.

And if I might add, how egotistical are you in your drive to assert your viewpoint on to someone using that tone? Please lighten up, stand back and just shower the person with love instead. I know you mean well and you are not intending to be so ammunitious (verbally attacking) or to make our experiences more difficult for us. I understand your challenging our belief system is in your sincere effort to help us; you really want us to be happy. But you must know, listening to you actually creates the opposite effect.

When a baby learns to walk and falls, no one yells and says, "Use your other foot to prevent yourself from falling! It's your own fault you're falling down. Get up! What's wrong with you? I'm trying to tell you how to stand on two feet why can't you listen!" No, instead, we say, "Uh–oh---, try it again sweetie." The toddler does not have the brain capacity to understand the concept of, "Use your other foot…"; all the child understands is the tone of your voice and the energy behind it. In such a situation, the baby would feel bad, cry and develop a negative sense of self if the yelling continued over time.

At some point within the toddler's development, an understanding of how to navigate herself around a room does arise and before long, the little one is not only standing and walking but is also able to pivot. Later, she is able to run or hop on one foot. But these motor skills do not happen before the brain develops in a way that would allow for those abilities to take place.

While we all physically grow at a slow pace, growth in our consciousness also takes baby steps. When we put one foot before the other, it's like developing the ability to place one concept as a building block to enable us to grasp another. Some people are able to make leaps in their ability to understand ideas. Most of us are just regular folk; we have to take one step at a time. Some of us have to sit with concepts for a while and sometimes stew over them before we are motivated to move forward. This trouble we make for ourselves is usually unconscious and when we wake up to the fact that we don't have to be miserable, we start the business of learning how to get past the misery. With all that being said, those of us who don't get it need the same "Try it again sweetie, I am here for you" attitude as does a toddler who is starting to learn to walk. Until then, we only feel bad about ourselves and start to add to the negative self-perception we already have. If you really want to help, have some patience; our brain has not yet made the necessary leap to understand you.

Love is what did it for me; it helped me to understand how I created my world as I learned how consciousness creates our reality. Love from higher beings around me, just when I needed it most, gave me permission to lighten up. I became able to take a step back and ease up on myself. This caused me to relax and forgive myself, to just accept where I was: in the dark. Love enabled me to see I am not the bad person others made me out to be by blaming me with such strong convictions out loud and in public. Those who have not had an awakening are a work in progress, and no amount of rushing them is going to make it happen any sooner. They have to do it at the speed of which they are capable. So back off and give them some room to grow at their own pace and abilities. When people like me come to you and talk to you about their problems, they don't need a slap in the face of reality from you at that time. What is needed is an understanding that this is the method to their madness and at some point, they will get it, but this is how they happen to be processing the journey in the moment.

At times, one friend simply would say things like, "I see that is a struggle for you; it must be frustrating." Other words that helped were, "I'm sorry you're having such a hard time right now. I will pray for you." These are the kinds of affirmations one needs to hear when going through a difficult time. Having this type of attitude toward us helps us to take a breath and gives us the space to dig deeper for the truth. So, give us a break; we have already beaten ourselves up and your smack down feels like putting the last bit of dirt over the grave that we feel we are lying in.

There will be a time when we will also get tired of hearing the stories we tell. I sure did, and while it was a slap in the face, it was self-inflicted. I began to hear myself speak about all the terribleness of my life and it sounded like I was on a megaphone when it happened. The words I spoke were piercing and bounced back at me with such a force it felt like a beating. "Wow! I shouted. Is this the crap I've been reciting all those years?" I could almost smell rubber burning as I abruptly put on the breaks and stopped telling the accounts of my life. I realized, "DAMN! I finally get it now." My constant recitation of my struggles is what created the misery in my life. I had to come to this on my own. No amount of others yelling or getting poked in the chest got me there. I could not have arrived at this point without patience and loving kindness from people who were untouched by my evils. It seemed they knew what I was up against and offered their compassion. So, an awakening will come. Be patient. For some, telling their story again and again might be what's needed before they can see daylight.

Simply allow your friend to go through their own unraveling and be a witness to it while offering hugs or kind words of support; you don't have to stick around if you don't want. But when you are in the presence of a mind in midst of an alteration, have some patience and empathy. Just knowing you were there for a few minutes is just what's needed to not feel so terribly isolated in the thick of it. Offer the faith and a belief that she will get through this and come through to the other side.

Chapter II

Transformation and Glimpses of Higher States of Consciousness

"Enlightenment will be had by all."

The journey towards an ultimate state of consciousness doesn't always render a life of drama. Sometimes, our path can present something really special for us; we may have glimpses of self-realization. What if we only experience these sneak previews because our mind and body lack the synchronicity to support a sustained bliss? If the intellect and the physiology were developed in such a way, would we then have the ability to hold on to this altered state for the long term? It seems as though we have to have a mental and/or physical metamorphosis in order to do so.

When I reflect on this phenomenon, I compare the experience to looking at a faucet that is cranked back on after the utility company has turned off the water supply. When you turn your faucet on again, there is the alternate occurrence of a loud, disturbing noise and actual water. But before long, all you will notice is water flowing out. I'm guessing you have already understood the clear water to be the representation of higher states of awareness, and the clatter, the struggles along the way. When you look at what is going on with you, for example, it's easy to consider the body/mind theory I'm proposing. As you navigate through sometimes debilitating challenges on your journey, you are met with mental, and I would guess, physical complaints of deep stress. With all this in mind, it would be easy to assert the idea and say that it's true. Until we do the dirty work of clearing the pipe of all of our mental noise and its resulting physical debris, we will only have glimpses. They are what's in store for us when we let go of all that blocks our ability to see the truth within ourselves.

My transformation over the years includes many signs that speak to the synchronicity of the mental, physical and psychic aspects of my being. On the physical level, there are occasional headaches. At times, there is electrical current rushing up my back and sometimes other parts of my body. In the third eye area, there is throbbing when I sit to meditate. Psychologically and psychically, I'm experiencing an urgency to do whatever I can to help others in need. Other times, there is so much mental fogginess, I can't even focus. Sometimes I see lights flashing in front of me, and I hear music and tones that seem to have no place of origin. Also, my senses have become heightened. When I am playing the stereo, for example, and singing to the top of my lungs, I can feel the phone ringing. I can hear things others don't hear until a few seconds later or smell aromas that also seem to come from nowhere. And recently, I discovered the ability to understand a language I don't even speak. Though it's not a regular occurrence, I am baffled by this gift. My dreams are lucid with the power to manipulate what happens in them. I feel awake while sleeping, and I am often aware of what is happening around me.

As I visited doctors, my symptoms have been unexplained by blood tests and scans. I have a clean bill of health yet my experiences continue. Some may argue these physical events are the byproduct of foods I'm eating. With food becoming more and more suspect for

11

ailing the physical body, human or otherwise, it's a good argument. But I have been a vegetarian for over 15 years and have eaten vegan and organic foods for the past eight years. I also make sure to get all nutritional needs met by supplementing my diet with whole vitamins and minerals as needed, so I trust it's not about what I put into my body. If you have experienced some or all the above indications and you doubt it relates to an awakening, see a doctor to make sure you are not experiencing these symptoms due to a medical problem.

As far as glimpses go, if the mind and body do have to synchronize to allow us permanent higher states of consciousness, then the time it happens would be totally subjective. This is because it would depend on your own physiology and your own psyche as well as life experiences. No one would know when your moment will occur, not even you. I also believe all people will become self-realized regardless of one's physical or mental abilities, race, and lifestyle or how little or much prayer is performed. No matter your spiritual endeavors or the lack thereof, enlightenment will be had by all. But I have to say, going inward is the way to go. Such a daily routine comes with many benefits and can boost your understanding and knowledge about life, to say the least.

I experienced a profound understanding about my life while in the throes of a depressive state of mind. It was in the middle of the night, and I couldn't sleep. Tears were streaming down my face as I felt suicidal and became anxious. Because I really didn't want to die, I picked up an old book and started reading it from the beginning one more time. I decided to give myself another chance at my life. You might ask if I am enlightened. The answer: not by any imaginative stretch. I am just someone who has become aware of my many issues. I have become able to tune in to old thought and behavior patterns that have wrecked my life. And I have realized the importance of changing my mind in order to eradicate them.

Many of us have an awakening process that can involve a time of depression. This state of mind often includes thoughts and/or actions of suicide attempts. It can be a trial when we feel mentally unstable and can experience moments of anxiety that last for varying periods of time. There are nights when you cannot sleep, or you feel the need to sleep more, usually during the day. You may feel exhausted or have a change in appetite during this stage. It's not uncommon during depression to experience episodes of crying due to feeling overwhelmed with sadness. If you were asked what bothers you, an answer wouldn't come. This is because you wouldn't know where to start if someone gave you the attention.

Times like these can be a place in our consciousness where we doubt that we are on the right path. We begin to question the validity of almost everything of a spiritual nature. Our friends and family may start to worry about us. Loved ones begin to question your sanity or need for medication and counseling as they see you behaving out of character. You don't have to go through this ordeal alone. If you are in this state of mind, you could benefit from seeing a counselor for emotional support, someone who can help you put things into perspective. Give yourself another chance; you deserve it.

Chapter III

Train Wreck

*"Because of the negative thoughts
we choose to believe, no one
can make us suffer any more
than we make ourselves."*

ike many 14-year-old kids, I couldn't wait to become an adult. I was anxious to get my own living space and to pursue my dreams of being a psychologist and a scientist. I also wanted a car so I could go and come as I saw fit without the adults holding the reigns to my freedom. As an adolescent, I wasn't a rebel but I did question authority; there were so many things I wanted and needed to know. As a young girl, I did my best not to fall out of line as I was either too shy or too terrified of my grandparents to misbehave. Before she passed away, my grandmother served as a deacon in the church and everyone in the house would attend services three to four times a week. The other adults were choir members or played other integral roles in the small two-story building. I didn't like going to church much. What I experienced at home and what I heard from the pastor during worship were inconsistent and my elders never seemed to get it right.

By the time I was old enough to graduate from high school, I had the ambition beat out of me along with a playful spirit I had inherited from my mother. I was numb and somewhat self-destructive, a mess as I began abusing alcohol. I had no plans to go to college right away. But when I finally did attend, I saw a poster on my way to class. There tacked on to a tree was a flyer that led me to something wonderful: Transcendental Meditation, ™. I went to the introduction session and the following initiation ceremony. When I got my mantra, I transcended as I sat down and closed my eyes; I finally had peace of mind. Whenever I practiced this technique, I felt like God descended on to me. Even in daily activities I felt profound peace. By the time I was 27 years old, I was well into adulthood, working, mothering, paying bills and shopping for my one-bedroom apartment; I was happy and felt successful in my life.

But I had also started a drinking career a few years before my daughter was born. With the help of dry tasting wines and malt liquors, I managed to suppress those areas of my psyche I felt best left alone. I gave up the habit when I learned I was pregnant. But when my daughter turned two years old, I fell into old behaviors again. I could blame the stress of single parenting and the total lack of support from anyone for falling off the wagon. The 40 hour work week, commuting to the baby sitter by bus, then to work and that in reverse after the day was done, was exhausting. Doing it all again the next day wore a hole in my ability to function. Life became a crazy rat race I didn't think I had signed up for; there was hardly any time to transcend. And if that wasn't enough, as my daughter grew, memories of my horrible childhood surfaced and became unbearable. Finally, I decided to see a committed therapist. And after many years of hard work, I was able to manage my life as a survivor of childhood abuse as well as that which I encountered as an adult. I attended an Alcoholics Anonymous group a few times a week as I decided I was worth a life of sobriety. Besides, my daughter needed a mother that was present and responsible.

After some time, I had achieved over 30 years of sobriety. This fact seemed to not matter because my world was still a train wreck. Everything around me was collapsing with every step I took. I kept getting fired from jobs and would end up homeless. None of these things happened when I drank. I watched documentaries claiming that life can be great as long as you believe and have the right attitude. The hosts of these programs would stress, "Visualize and it's yours." I watched those shows over and over just in case I missed something -- I wanted to get it right. I'm a recovering perfectionist too, you see. I wanted to live like I believed and wanted my environment to be a living proof that I had it right. The truth is, I wanted people to be in awe of me. So, I was always on a self-improvement trip.

Some of the spiritual books I studied were written by enlightened men and women. Reading them wasn't the only assistance to my spiritual growth. I prayed every day and not just for my good but also for the sake of others. I fasted one day a week while meditating for long hours. I donated art to charity, raised money for the homeless; the list isn't too long but long enough to warrant some good in my life, though I did not expect anything in return for helping others.

Loving friends became enemies for reasons they did not bother to share, and no matter how I tried to hold on to my best friend of 14 years, I realized finally, it was best for me to just let her go. I didn't mean to drag those closest to me into the realm of my hellish life. But by bitching and moaning about one thing after another,

I unknowingly projected my negative energy. Who in their right mind would hang around such darkness? Though I miss them terribly, I don't blame them for leaving.

There were times I would be accused by strangers of things I didn't do. I had just boarded a plane in Germany for example, and as soon as I sat down, a woman already seated accused me of stealing her bracelet, one I received from my guru. There was a time when I was physically assaulted. Twice in the same week, a car ran into my car. And as a pedestrian, I was even hit by a woman who wasn't paying attention. Life became a mystery, a nightmare that had been continuing for the larger portion of my existence. Many therapists would drop me, never to call me back or to show up to the appointments they would set for me. I would be stood up, and when I confronted them, they blamed me for misunderstanding the time of my next visit. I didn't have the guts to go to them with the appointment cards they gave me; after each session I received a reminder of the next appointment date, proof that I wasn't the one who made the mistake.

One would think my life was great. After all, I meditated twice a day and had been doing so for over three decades. But in 2006, those blissful experiences I got from T.M. vanished suddenly. I kept up the practice for two more years out of habit, I guess, before throwing it away all together.

I became so depressed that all I could see was failure and darkness in and around me. Suicide was a constant thought, and at times, I got so close to killing myself. There was a period of great sadness in January 2014, a time when I felt I had had it with this life. I was serious; I wanted out and had a plan of action. I was tired of being alone, broke and without friends. I felt I had every reason to leave this planet. Instead of acting on my thoughts, I became aware of a very quiet voice inside my head. It was a voice I had heard many times before but had lost it somehow. It was the stillness of the inflection that got my attention. It had no anxiety or a mood of depression. It felt soft, compassionate yet stern. A voice that suggested I pick up my favorite self-help book. When I did, I pored over the pages unlike I ever had. I read it with an open mind and focused on the message in a way I had never done. I had no preconceived notions on where a sentence was taking me. My mind was completely open without judgment or without the need to file concepts with the scheme of things already in my head. I felt my mind take in each word as if it was the first time I had picked up the book. And in the middle of the text, an understanding came over me that related to the events about my life. I had come to realize it was I who caused myself so much unhappiness. And it was in that moment I felt a peace come over me. And all of a sudden, I became relieved of my suffering. Finally, I got it. What followed was answers to all the lifelong questions for which I had desperately longed. Why was I so unhappy? Why did I feel so stuck? Why hadn't I achieved the things I had set out to do? More and more of them were answered as they flooded back into my awareness in what seemed like a second's time. Sheer happiness, bliss and a profound sensation of being fully present took hold of me. While this feeling seems to come and go, I am confident it is never really gone. My friend Gabrielle calls those moments, "The silence of serenity," times when I am in bliss and grinning from ear to ear.

Before I had that wonderful experience in 2014, people were confronting me about my attitudes. I didn't care that they would call me self-righteous. I would reflect and then tell them they were wrong. I was the Shit who knew it all. Yet with all I knew, I was still unhappy in the worst way, a struggle that epitomized suffering. It was the year before my epiphany when the rope I was holding on to began to fray, threatening to snap at any moment. When it finally broke, I became airborne without the possibility of a soft landing. I was holding on so tightly to everything I thought I knew; I didn't realize this behavior wasn't serving me. Acquaintances called me stubborn, but I didn't think I was until I found myself in pieces, climbing out of a hole I unknowingly dug for myself. I didn't realize how hopeless I was. I just didn't understand.

Chapter IV

The Continued Struggle

*"The challenges we face in life,
happen only to make us strong and to
promote reality within ourselves."*

After meeting my present guru in 2006, I again lost jobs which rendered me homeless and walking aimless while hanging out on the streets. There were times I slept in my car if I had one or on a stranger's sofa. Not too long ago, I lived in a friend's office where he worked in some remote part of the small town in which I lived -- what a frightening experience when the sun set. All the things that could go bump in the night actually went bump while the building was settling. I slept so little because of it.

In 2013, I lost my mother four days before Mother's Day. Five months later, my father also died. I couldn't understand why all this was happening. I thought I was a positive person and that good things happened to positive people. While I wrote out daily gratitude lists, visualized my highest good, asked for and expected the best, I got NOTHING. You can imagine the feelings of disappointment and frustration that resulted.

As I did all the praying and chanting, horrible things would manifest instead. In other words, desires didn't just not materialize as I was told to expect. I was met instead with some creepy, negative forces of energy whenever I did my spiritual practices. It was as if I was being forced, on some psychic level, to just give up my quest for the light, and I almost did, many times. Not that I was going to join the dark forces; I was just going to give up all hopes of ever reaching my goal of enlightenment or being happy, for that matter. At this point, I felt God hated me for a sport, that the almighty loved making me miserable.

When new potential friends came around, they would challenge my approach to life and blame me for all the misfortune that was, as I put it, "happening to me." How insensitive of them, I thought, to say I created the lengthy chain of events that destroyed everything I ever had or reached for. I thought I knew it all; like I said, I read the books and thought I was walking the talk.

I turned to astrology for answers. I began to run into others of the same sign who were in exactly the same situations: friendless, homeless and unemployed. But then I noticed there were plenty of us who are extremely successful. They are sometimes plastered on the big screens for months at the IMAX theaters. Then I came to the realization that it couldn't be the astrological sign that was to blame for the craziness that was my life. In fact, I later read people of my planetary configurations had the King Midas touch, that is, everything they put their hands on turned to gold. Well, I saw no support to this claim in my life.

I had great ideas about how to help troubled teens. I also wanted to promote love on the planet by way of offering workshops in different cities. Working in these areas would allow me some autonomy. I wanted to move about and not sit in place at a desk; I had too much energy for that. However, there was nothing I could do to implement these plans. No one would return phone calls or emails and money would not manifest that would afford these dreams. And when I spoke of my plan to help the world in this way, some thought it was a really good idea, but others would just look at me as if I had lost my mind for sure. I had zero support of nature in my effort to promote change large or small in the world.

I was blind to my own limitations; I thought I could do anything I put my mind to. There's no doubt this is still the case, but there was so much inner healing I needed to do first. I realized I could not help direct the masses on how to love if I felt unloved. All my personal problems screamed volumes about how I knew nothing about the subject, so what could I offer anyone? This is why nature was not supportive of my ideas to start women's groups. There were no responses to the letters sent as I wrote to prospective sponsors and to other women's organizations in the country. Finally, I came to understand no matter how much determination you have to accomplish something, if you do not have the inner foundation in place to support those actions you aspire to perform, your outer world will not materialize. You will only spend many years longing for your dreams to come true.

If a woman wants to become an electrician, she would have to have the principles of electronics in her knowledge bank. If a man wanted to play the role of a pick-pocket in a movie, he would have to understand the mindset of one. The actor would have to know how such a thief moves about in a way so as to not be noticed in order to play the part well. By the same token, I wasn't psychologically prepared to form groups and direct members on how to project love. My goal was to instruct them to first love themselves and then direct them on how to spread this feeling throughout the country. I had done my research; I had a business plan and a list of possible contacts in various cities as well as other projects in place to make it happen. But I first needed to have a foundation of love and truth in place within myself. Having these qualities would have allowed for those gatherings to manifest. For me it seemed I was ready to run when I had not yet learned how to walk. It was as if I fell into being and was ready to start on the divine plan without first checking to see what tools I had at my disposal. I just wanted to get the crazy parts of my life over so I could make a change in the world. And it seemed like the craziness would never dissolve. It's not that I pretended to have no weaknesses; I was just tired of the world passing me by without my input. I so much wanted to help promote some good on the planet. I also wanted to be where the people were who made things happen globally. But I was so wrapped up in all my drama, there was no way I could pull off such a feat. I simply had no inner references to draw from that would qualify me to start and complete the project. I had nothing to work with.

How was I going to act globally when on a small scale, I could hardly keep up with my own life? This madness I had been going through for so long was a relentless distraction. Every time I turned around, some birthday or holiday was in the now. In other words, I had no awareness of needing to buy a card or save up to purchase gifts or festive food to share. The stress of rushing out to acknowledge the occasion added to the distraction as it left me feeling inept. My daughter would call to ask what we were doing for the Fourth of July for example, and because my mind was so scattered, I was not aware that one of the most exciting days of the year for her was fast coming. My lack of planning for the holidays meant I had not put money aside to do anything to make them special. At those times, I was often pouring small change out of jars or checking seat cushions in order to buy something to cook. But now that I have done some amount of healing, I have become aware of annual events long before the calendar clues me in. I've also come to realize, working on myself is a good place to start when I think about affecting the world on a grand scale. As you begin to heal, you too will find you are no longer distracted by the events of your life. You will have the ability to acknowledge the important dates of those around you as you climb out of your hole to join the living.

Chapter V

After All You've Done

"While you may feel as though you have lost your mind, you are actually gaining awareness."

Many who walk a spiritual path fall into a belief that they are without fault; they can do no wrong. Such a life would mean that one holds the attitude of love and respects all living creatures unconditionally, which also include one's self. It also means that you behave according to those beliefs. Truth seekers know the language that describes how individuals should, and therefore, also how they should not, live their lives. Not that they all go out preaching to the world, but they strive to read everything written by the sages. They have studied all the DVDs that either through audio or visual prompts, direct a life of fulfillment. Those on a spiritual path enjoy gathering with those of like mind while praying, reading scripture, socializing, and comparing stories. You can see them at lectures, taking notes, and soaking up the vibes of "good energy" at random or scheduled meetings.

All of this devotional activity offers us a good feeling as it reinforces our belief system. Being with those who think like us renders an opportunity to see our growth and to try out new attitudes. From them, we also take in new information and discover new insights, but only if it fits in with our present constructs. If the new information doesn't gel with what you already believe, you tend to throw it out in fear of a challenge to your old and limited way of thinking.

You may find you are not progressing. Maybe you think you are even backtracking on your journey to the light. "I pray every day and still get no satisfaction. Why does my life suck?" you may ask. You may also wonder what you are doing wrong. You think somewhere you made a wrong turn; you figured you must have because otherwise, your life would not be filled with such god awful misery. You leave the house on time, for example, to catch your bus to class or work and in the very moment you walk around the corner, it has just left the stop. You have been volunteering for the poor each time you are called to do so, and yet at the office, your boss won't give you a raise that is long overdue. You fight with your loved ones, and the neighbors suddenly cannot stand the sight of you. Somehow you fell out of synchronicity with nature and your life seems to be spiraling out of control. Though you try, there seems to be nothing you can do to fix it. All the chanting, meditation, and going to church every Sunday offers you no relief. Some of you may have even yelled, "WHAT IN THE HELL IS GOING ON?"

Such an existence can make you question the powers that be and just drop your quest all together. "Why should I stay on a path if all I get is crap thrown in my face at every turn?" "Why take time out of my already stressful day to perform practices that are not benefiting me?" "SCREW IT! I DON'T NEED THIS SHIT!" Next, all the pictures and candles that make up your alter get taken down and thrown into a box; you stop going to church or other similar gatherings. Spiritual or religious texts get either thrown on a closet shelf or donated to a thrift store. You find yourself thinking, "What's the use, I'll never amount to anything anyway. Years and years of facing God and all I get is this? What's the use?"

Feeling this way may cause you to try to escape the pain by getting wrapped up in senseless activity, you know, like watching those popular TV shows. You do this as if your life depended on it while staring at the screen in a daze. Some develop unhealthy eating habits or other addictions. You may start to think anything at all to numb your pain would be sufficient. At some point in your loneliness you start to reminisce on how much fun it was to fellowship with other members of your spiritual group. You think back on how great you felt during those rare moments when you felt bliss sweep up on you during prayer or other practices. You begin to cry because you cannot believe after all those years, you still feel like a loser and that your life reflects just that. Anger builds up inside but it's no relief when you finally explode. You can't help but feel you have wasted all of your time worshiping for nothing. You curse God and wonder why you deserve such treatment. You vow never to put foot on the path again as it has brought you nothing but sheer pain and agony. You have labored over Bible verses trying to extract their deepest meaning. Some of you can recite scripture in your sleep. Others of you have sat in the most uncomfortable postures for hours expecting to transcend into higher states of consciousness. You have been re-birthed, hypnotized, have been saved, baptized, born again, initiated, and sanctified. Still, you find yourself stuck in some black hole that won't spit you out, a void that has left you feeling so empty and alone inside, you can't remember the last time you were genuinely happy. You have lost the closest of friends, the best jobs, your house, your car, and if that wasn't enough, your cell phone fell into the toilet. Your world as you know it is a mess and for the life of you, you can't figure out how it got that way.

Some question their own existence and try suicide as a way out. Others just don't respond to life at all anymore; they sit catatonic on street corners or in psych wards. Yet some of you are die-hards; you don't give up. You keep searching for reasons things are the way they are or ways to make your lives better. You are probably not listening to others who try to assist but you do keep searching, looking for a way out. Some people around you may scream and point to the exit but you don't hear them because you're either too busy telling them "I know" or you're just too belligerent and who wants to be around that?

Take A Moment to Connect
With Your Body and Mind

Take three deep breaths; slowly in, slowly out. Relax. Feel the coolness of your breath as you inhale. Feel the warmth as you move the air out through your nostrils. Next, breathe normally, taking unaltered breaths. Now that you have your own attention, can you feel your brain processing all of this information? How are you feeling? Are you anxious, feeling hopeless or uncertain? Take some time and have a look inside to see what's going on. Now that you have just assessed your mind, let's turn the attention to other areas of your being. How does your body feel? Focus on your feet, legs, thighs, and hips. Take a moment and just pay attention to those regions. How about your pelvic area, abdomen and lower back; what are they holding on to? Whatever it is, let it go. Can you feel any sensations? If not, take all the time you need to feel the energy in all of these areas. You may feel some tingling, spasms or some other sensations. What about your stomach, what impression are you getting from it? Does it gurgle, hurt, or burn; what is it telling you? Now, focus on the middle back area and chest. Get a sense of your chest rising and collapsing with each breath you take. Notice your heart beating; does it pump fast or slow? When you place your attention onto your hands, wrist, lower and upper arms are you flexing your muscles in anticipation, or are they relaxed? Feel whatever is happening in these areas of your body. How are your shoulders, and neck;

are they tight or do they hurt? Just take some time to feel and to be in your body. It's OK to be in your body. Now, back to your head, what's going on there? Is it throbbing? Are you dizzy or does your head feel just fine? After you have scanned your body in this way, take a few more minutes before picking up your book. Just be here now. At this time, have no description of how you feel, just observe the moment while being present. Take all the time you need with this process.

Chapter VI

Possible Reasons: Get This

"As long as we believe negatively about the events in our lives, we will continue to experience life according to those beliefs as a result."

worried so much about everything. Then, I came to understand that when I agonize over the things in my life, the universe thinks I am making a request. You see, when we think, we are actually praying; prayers are the contents of our thoughts. So, when we start thinking negatively or worrying (whatever you want to call it in a troubled or lower state of consciousness), the universe is listening because that is what it does. All it knows how to do is respond in kind to what we speak or think; it matches a response to a request. When you worry about not having decent clothes or enough food to eat, the universe listens closely and matches that thought and makes a delivery to you on a silver platter, the representation of those thoughts in the material form. The universe listens intently to everything you say and everything you think because that's its job. It sets out to mirror those thoughts and words and gives them back to you in a relevant form; it wants to reflect your every thought, verbal or otherwise.

And if that is not enough, if you are very emotional with your thoughts or speech, your wish may materialize in record speed. It doesn't matter if you are thinking positively or negatively, since the universe doesn't know the difference between the two; it wants to give you everything about which you think or speak.

When the delivery shows up, and it's not to our favor, we get frustrated, angry, and throw our hands up screaming, "Why, God?" At some point, the universe does not support you anymore because it seems not to know what else to do. It gave you everything you could think of, (which of course included the misery you projected). What then is the creator to do but stop supporting you? Not even your good thoughts are returned because the universe is mirroring how confused you are. When we cannot decide on one thing versus another, we get absolutely nothing. When we speak of the good things we feel we deserve and then in the next sentence or the next day, tell our sob stories, we are being indecisive. If the universe could talk back, it might say something like this:

> *Wait a minute, didn't you just make a request for something (i.e., spoke of how good things are)? Now, you are making another request (i.e., telling your sob stories). And no matter what it is you ask of me, I deliver and you are still unhappy. I don't know what you want, I am confused. I give up!"*

When we keep telling the universe we want good things while continuing to speak about the negativity in our lives, we get absolutely nothing. No nature support, no return of good deeds, no money to fix the car, no ride to the mall. NOTHING. All we get is the negativity we project, getting nothing good in return as a result. Does this make sense?

Before my epiphany, I was spending so much time being angry. And I could not think without feeling some form of cynicism. I became very bitter about life and the sense of humor I once had turned into sour jokes that never made it to the punch line. With every experience I considered bad, I developed a bad attitude and of course a story that told it all. I did not understand rehashing the negative accounts of my life over and over and over again only reinforced the negative experiences I was having. In fact, telling my pathetic stories perpetuated more sob stories to tell. With all my complaining, I didn't realize I was actually giving the universe a list of negative experiences to deliver. Then I embellished that craziness flowing back to me with emotion and a bad outlook on my life and the people in it. After a while, this resulted in depression, which spun into a life filled with misery and suffering, which created more bad experiences by way of my constantly talking about it, which.......

Now do you understand how you got into your wreck? I hope so, because it took me the better part of my 59 years to understand that whatever I thought, I experienced its matching results or consequences. Whatever I sowed, I would reap. As I had negative thoughts, I continuously created a negative situation to match it and it became a habit to think in this way. As you create unfortunate circumstances, you start to believe negatively about your life. And as you believe negatively about the events in your life, you live according to those beliefs as a result of creating through thought.

Chapter VII

What Do You Really Know?

"Understand that in any situation in life, there is someone who is further along than we are, in the same boat or just a little behind us on our journey."

" know;" "I already Know;" "I already read that one, in fact, I could have written it myself;" "I have already seen that one." Sounds like you? A know-it-all really does not know it all. Otherwise, no one would have to tell such a person anything, ever. If this is your life, then you have a lot more to understand. Let's face it, if you have done a lot of spiritual practices and you find you are still playing the role of Sisyphus, the truth is, you really don't know much at all. It is time you put into practice those things you have read or viewed. To know something is to live it and all you have done was intellectualize what you've studied.

Now, one way I managed to get my consciousness lifted was to just listen without "I know" blocking my hearing. I decided to open myself up to the possibility of not knowing a thing. When I wasn't listening, I was missing out on something that could have awakened me. Advice from others may have sounded redundant, but those same words might have been said in a way that could have unlocked something inside of me, causing me to get it. But because I wasn't listening, I didn't hear how the words were spoken so I remained in the dark.

Sometimes we don't grasp things the first time we hear them. After all, that is why you are reading this book. It's not that we are of lower intelligence, because most of us are so damn smart. We just get in our own way. We are so in our heads, always analyzing things down to the minutest level. We try to fit new knowledge into what we already know. And we like to weigh the pros and cons when making decisions. But, we have to listen. We have to let people tell us information again to give ourselves a chance to take it in further. What if familiar words were spoken with a different feeling behind them? That feeling could give those comments the power to reach deeper inside of us, freeing us as it finally resonates, like when I read Eckhart Tolle one more time. When I did, my mind expanded. I saw lights floating around my apartment. There were bright lights flashing and floating about the living room. Everything looked brand new and crystal clear. I felt air in my brain as if something in my head had become dislodged. Hearing information you have heard before can be a trigger that could lead you to have more clarity. This clarity could be the impetus that could open you up somehow and cause you to finally get it.

Instead of saying "I know," you could face the person in front of you, have eye contact and apologize for not listening. Ask them to repeat the message while you drop your defenses and let their words sink in. So often we feel like we have to stand up for ourselves; we seem to do so without reason. Some of us have been abused as kids. As a result, we feel the need to create a one man army in our defense against the world. While growing up, we may have had to do so much on our own because those who were supposed to take care of us were not available. Lord knows they did what they could but it left us to our own devices. By the time we become adults, we may feel like those who have hurt us aren't the only ones against us. We have come to believe the whole world is our enemy. We have acquired so much life experience and so much knowledge as a result of growing up prematurely. As children, we knew things others just had not yet learned.

Today you feel you have made good choices in life and have lived honestly. In this mindset, you can't see the mistakes you make. In the past, you couldn't make them; there was no room for error. You were a child and had to fend for yourself and/or your siblings. And when you took on that caregiver role as a child, you never fell out of character. As adults, we are still that little girl or little boy who just wants confirmation that we did alright. Well, I want you to know, you did just fine. You made it this far, and you did a great job of looking out for yourself and hanging in there. Because you feel bad about yourself, you are not able to realize you are still heading forward. You haven't taken a wrong turn. Understand that no matter how you feel, our souls are always heading towards enlightenment. Pain is part of growth. What you are experiencing now won't last because the nature of life is ever changing, moment by moment.

It's time to unclench your fist, take some deep breaths, get up and keep stepping. Your life is not over yet. You don't have to lie down and play dead in hopes the world will just leave you alone. Besides, behaving in this way hasn't worked, has it? Make some changes instead, a change of mind, if you will. New thought processes followed by a change in behavior are in order. So if you want to reap the benefits of spirituality, let down your guard; no one is knowingly trying to hurt you or make you feel bad. If you listen long enough to those who are trying to help you, at some point, you will begin to realize they mean you no harm. Granted, some are pretty brutal with their presentation, but maybe that's what is needed to get you to listen for a change. People care about you but they get frustrated and do the best they can in those situations.

Open your mind and ears. Put aside all the impulses that tell you to say "I know" and relax. If hearing people's directions for achieving a better life feels like a threat, then be courageous. Keep your chin up and take on the challenge; it will help you grow. What have you got to lose?

Can you learn new information if you're running your mouth or playing old thought and behavior patterns? And push pause on the self-pity tape too, by the way, and just kick back and listen. Now, I ask you, if you are floating in the middle of the Pacific Ocean, would you reach out for an inflated raft if someone threw you one? Maybe you are someone who would continue swirling around in salt water stewing about your problems. If you are one who would take the raft, read on.

So often, we don't even see the help people offer. We are blind to the answer that is in front of us. We dismiss it because "I know" gets in the way. You may bitch and moan about how the boss man gave your parking spot to the new guy, though you have been an employee for many years. You cry about all the bills that need to be paid and not having enough money to cover them. And you say you can't for the life of you make definitive decisions about what you want to do to improve your status as a human being.

"Do this" or "try that" are suggestions you may hear from those who have stuck by you through it all. Yet your response to them is, "What do you know?" You may not say it verbally, but every time you keep struggling and complaining about how much you are struggling, you may as well have yelled it in their ears. You could lose your friends; after all, who wants to be around a miserable self-righteous know it all? "I know" just won't let you be happy. "I know" wants you to suffer so that you can get others to join in on your pity party. Well, look around; you are the only one in attendance.

You may think you are not seeking the attention of others by crying and complaining. But why else would you keep protesting about how life treats you? It's OK to want help with a problem. But when friends reach out and offer you sound advice, you don't listen. Instead of considering their help, the words "I know already" get in your way. And when you get by yourself, you ask: "What do they know? I'm the one who dissected philosophical texts in the wee hours of the night, and have gone to the workshops that keep me in the know. Where do they get off telling me what to do? I'm the one who facilitated a spiritual group, not them." The "I know" syndrome has you deep in its claws and it will take some effort to break free but only if you really want to be happy.

"I know" is an eraser that for some destroys their whole lives and even themselves. All your hopes and dreams can vanish. POOF! I used to think living as an alcoholic erased your life away but the "I know" disease does so with equal venom. Sufferers of this condition get sucked up into a vacuum, leaving them in pieces, feeling empty, lonely, confused and deceived. It can also cause feelings of disillusion, helplessness, fear and spiritual burnout. Feelings of worthlessness, along with mental exhaustion, are also common in this state of mind. It takes away your ability to have rational thought and can literally cause insanity on the road inward. Having "I know" can also spawn diseases in your body. Usually those who know it all have physical ailments to prove it. They sometimes feel as though the whole world is against them and may take issue with everything and everybody. There is no pleasing them because no one but themselves can ever do anything the right way. And no one knows quite as much as they know.

Isn't it lonely, knowing so much and having so little if anything to show for it? Some of you may still have your material possessions or circle of friends. However, if you are traveling towards enlightenment and have the symptoms listed on these pages, give it time. Your "I know" disorder may at some point leave you hanging by a thread. No one wants to be around someone who chronically complains about their life. No one wants to be around all that negative energy, certainly not spiritual folk.

Complainers often ask themselves, "Why is this happening to me? I just donated $100 to the food pantry last Christmas. Hell, I even spent 14 hours last week volunteering for hospice." It seems like no matter how much good you do in the world, your life seems to lack the karma that reflects all you do for others. I can almost hear you cry, "It's not fair!"

You are a good person, and at times this is what people tell you. You do whatever you can to help those less fortunate than you. Though you give your time and money you find somehow you still come up with the short end of the stick. You are exhausted and want out, yet you don't know which way to turn. Usually when individuals are going through rough times in their lives, they turn to God for answers. Who do you get to turn to when you feel God is the problem? What a horrible place to be, feeling like you are a never-ending drop of mud into a black hole.

Well, as mentioned before, sometimes we cannot see the light in front of our eyes. People are giving you suggestions but you unconsciously choose not to hear; you choose to stay in the dark. If this is you, you are suffering from what I call USB, secondary to the "I know" syndrome. I'm not writing about a wire used to hook up your computer, nor am I referring to a flash drive. USB stands for unconscious selective blindness. OK, I made this up but stay with me here. You see, the "I know" knows the light is there but it does not allow you to follow it. If you follow the truth about what ails you and heal, then the "I know" syndrome would fail to exist; the ego would become demolished as the two are one and the same.

There are a few possible reasons why you ignore the truth. One being, "I know" has you believing the light or truth that is trying to get your attention can hurt your feelings. You already feel bad and don't want to deal with more emotional discomfort. Also under the "I know" spell, you believe the light holder in front of you (at the time of your would-be rescue) is not qualified to tell you what to do to keep you from drowning. Your ego has you believing she has not done all you have done, read all you have read regarding the light. Maybe you think this person hasn't been to the places you have been to develop a level of spirituality it would take to save you. So you ask, "How could they possibly know what they are talking about?" You create in your mind a story about them that says they have not traveled on the spiritual path as long as you have or have not traveled at all.

In your weary mind, to take the light or to hear the truth they offer you would mean they know more than you. It would mean all your years of devotional inquiry, your sincere analysis of God's word, or all of your yoga practices meant nothing. In other words it would imply you still don't know enough. To you, it wouldn't be fair if someone who seems to put forth less effort in life reaped more benefit than you. Trust me, you are in no position to have USB when it relates to where your life-saver comes from. When the light bearers reach out to you, you pretend to swim instead, with a grin on your face saying, "Oh---I know, I got this." You can't fool those who offer a way out; they know you're in trouble but they are not going to keep extending themselves. Most of all, they are not going to stick around to watch you drown.

Be brave. Drop the notion that the light has to come from a holy person or someone who paid their dues, so to speak. Forget the truth has to come from someone who walked the path of righteousness or lived in ashrams or monasteries because it doesn't. It can come from someone who is older, someone younger or someone of a different race or creed than you. The light can come from anyone, even those of a different political affiliation than yours. Children are also channels of truth.

While you hold on so tightly to what you think you know, your attitude promises a crash landing; it doesn't offer any assistance out of your predicament. It's the light that shines your way out of ignorance, if you are brave enough to face it. And when you miss the opportunity to see the truth when it shines on you, there is no telling when the universe will offer you another chance any time soon. So have the courage and take it when it shows up in your life. Forget about what you know and run out of the darkness. Take the advice of spiritual travelers regardless of how long they have walked the path; for all you know, that person could actually be enlightened.

Understand that in any situation in life, there is always someone who is further along than we are, in the same boat or just a little behind us on our journey. Once we can get ourselves out of the way, we can begin to wake up to all the good that life has waiting for us. We can begin to benefit from all of our religious or spiritual endeavors. We can see that life does not have to be the struggle we once made it out to be. When we are met with obstacles, we can have a different understanding about them and use them as tools to help us flex our emotional muscle, that is, to give us the strength to do what it takes to meet life's demands. In addition, confronting our challenges head on furthers us along spiritually. We can begin the practice of changing our mind, our attitudes, by having more affirmative thoughts. When we take on a positive approach to life, it results in positive experiences. You've read other books or have watched documentaries on how to make such a change. It takes a constant and conscious effort in order to make the shift, but I know you can do it! One thing that helps me is the fact that whatever comes my way is not going to last forever, as everything changes. With this in mind, you can grow less and less attached to people, places and outcomes.

Chapter VIII

The Ego

"A desperate ego will do anything for attention. It doesn't matter if the attention is positive or negative."

Getting back to the ego, it can be a force to reckon with. And as mentioned before, it is sometimes indicated by the need to say "I know." The ego can also stand out as we strive for attention. Though you may deny it, you want recognition for all the good deeds you have done. You want to be known as the one to turn to, one who knows the answers. If you were to be acknowledged for all you know about everything, you would still be unhappy because the ego's thirst for praise is never quenched.

Your conceit has you thinking you are the shit; you would never admit it though, because you want people to think you are humble. Maybe you do so much for others because you have nothing else to do. If you had any friends, would you donate as much time to serving others? It doesn't mean you are not a good person, because you are. It just means you do it to reap the rewards, the attention that feeds your insatiable ME. When you don't get an ego boost, you whine instead about how no one appreciates you. Then that complaining flicks over the first domino of woes that sends the rest of the chain of complaints folding over one after another. The next thing you know, you are yapping about how you can't get any satisfaction, how disenchanted you are with your life.

And because of your unhappiness, you may feel the need to highlight the faults in others so as to distract yourself from fixing your own heap of troubles. You also focus on other people's shortcomings to make yourself feel better. Consider interrupting these behavior patterns as you drop your baggage of misery because they push your head further under water. When "I know" clouds your thinking, you can only see the faults of others. You're not able to see the flaws reflected within yourself.

Chapter IX

More on Behavior

"Hating others is a very effective way to show how much you really hate yourself, with 100% accuracy."

Like the "I know" syndrome, finger pointing is another thing that keeps us stuck. Feeling sorry for yourself, blaming others for your shortcomings, and taking revenge out on those with whom you find fault can also keep you stuck. Gossiping, putting other people down, and thinking you are superior: all of these behaviors stem from negative thought patterns and a poor sense of self. Besides, hating others is a very effective way to show how much you really hate yourself, with 100% accuracy.

When we are wallowing in self-pity, for example, we are begging, unconsciously or otherwise, for the attention of others. We are asking them to consider our circumstances as bleak and to help us. Most often, such a person would not accept the help because it would mean an end to all the attention they receive. At times you accept the advice but it's not long before more problems arise that require more care, and the drama starts again.

As a child, we may not have received enough positive attention from those on whom we depended. We developed creative ways to get what we needed from them. It may not have been the best way to get them to notice us but it worked. Because it worked, we kept doing it. Whining may have resulted in someone slapping us or yelling but at least they paid attention; we got them to look at us. And if that's not enough, we grew up still thinking nobody cares about us while we feel alone in our plight. Because we are human, we need others around us. When someone shows up, we start complaining; sometimes it doesn't matter with whom we are talking. We're hoping, "maybe **they** can give me answers." As a child, your parents would have guests from time to time. When those visitors showed up, you may have thought they would be able to help you or "maybe **they** will love me." When you reached out to them it didn't take long to realize the visitors were also inattentive.

Entertain this possibility: As adult chronic complainers, we don't complain for the hell of it. We are actually stuck in our childhood, asking to be acknowledged. It's as if we still need a hug from mommy and daddy. We need a glass of milk, someone to tie our shoe, or to be read to at bedtime. We simply want to know we matter. It's like we haven't grown up at all. Our needs are stuck in the past.

You may have heard this from somewhere before but I will express it again: It's not your fault you didn't get your needs met as a child. Whatever was going on with your parents or other adults in your childhood had nothing to do with you. Not loving you with all their heart is something they may regret. But today, you can be an adult. You can grow up and decide to love yourself despite what you learned as a child. While you had no control over your circumstances then, you can start anew by taking responsibility for what now happens to you.

We blame everybody else for our misfortune; we can't see how our behavior plays a part in how we are treated. We are blind to how our thoughts weave little pockets in our minds where we get stuck, places we go to lick our wounds and to hide. All we are aware of is the pain of having lost a job or the shock of totaling the car in an accident, for example. It is always the other person's fault; after all, "I am on a spiritual path, and the fault could not have been mine." "I know how to… (fill in the blank)." The message here is, you can do no wrong. In Alcoholics Anonymous, I learned that when you point a finger at another person, there are always more of them pointing your way. Take time right now and point. Don't you see? More fingers point back at you than at someone else; let that be a clue to where to place the cause of your problems.

Chapter X

The Wheel of Fortune

*"If we stopped to consider
how our thoughts affect us and
those around us, we might be
inspired to think differently."*

Revenge also stands in our way of experiencing a consciousness that is awake. Getting someone back for perceived wrongs they have done to us can be another way of blocking the gifts of God. You can sing sweet praises in the church choir on Sunday, but if you are plotting the demise of another, you may be inadvertently plotting your own hell. When considering the laws of karma, is it possible to hurt someone without also hurting yourself? Or is the old adage "What goes around, comes around" spoken to us just to keep us in line? If the saying is true, the law of cause and effect won't make any mistakes. You could write your own story of suffering if you consciously set out to harm another person. And that would include kicking your poor, defenseless cat.

You can set out to do harm even in thought. When we have demeaning thoughts, we bring negativity to ourselves; in this case, like attracts like. Also, if you are plotting to take revenge on someone, the dark energy of your unsupportive thoughts can make a prey out of you. You manifest whatever you think about. While it takes a constant effort, I find that being aware of what I think and practicing being present in every moment helps me to interrupt thoughts that are not favorable to life. And in case you forgot, what we think about contributes to the collective consciousness of the whole of mankind. When you become angry, you subscribe to war and other travesties in the world. I'm sure you didn't intend to help create the poor state of global affairs, but think of the ripple in the pond analogy. We forget sometimes that when we throw a pebble into the pond, the ripples pervade throughout the water and not just were the rock has landed.

Now that you have been reminded, you can do what you can to avoid counterproductive offers to global consciousness. Here is a technique I have learned from a world renowned sage and I am sure you too can master it: Next time you are fuming with emotion, you can slow down and focus on your breathing. Without altering it, be aware of your in and out breaths while being in the moment of your anger. Instead of acting on it, feel your body sensations. Notice how your heart is racing while the adrenalin rushes in to fuel your intentions. Feel your breath speeding up. Take notice of the sweat in the palms of your hands. Sometimes when we're angry, our face feels hot. Get in touch with all that your body feels in the moment of anger. Keep focusing on your breath and watch the feeling gradually dissipate into nothing. Being present is how you deal with your feelings of hatred, anger or any overwhelming emotion. By staying present, you can respond appropriately and bring some amount of peace to the collective mind, as well as your own.

When I think about the topic of revenge, I'm reminded of a bible verse I learned as a child: "Do unto others as you would have them do unto you." Now I have heard many versions of this advice since then that have nothing to do with turning the other cheek, as it were. "Do unto others as they do to you" is what's being recited by some. Did they hear the original quote, or are they just restating it to justify their momentary actions?

Instead of thinking about how we can harm others, let's think more about how to help them. Sacrificing ourselves in service results in more rewarding outcomes. In order to reap the benefit of good deeds, we have to perform good actions; you know this already. We also have to practice non-attachment. According to gurus and leaders like them, we should not expect to be rewarded for good behavior. They say we should do selfless service, not think about ourselves and what we will get out of good behavior. These guides say we should just stay in the present moment while giving our undivided attention to the service we are offering at the time. And I would like to add, when you offer your time to others and you are thinking of your reward, if your fate changes suddenly and your good karma runs out, how would you feel then? You would become very disappointed and disillusioned if you did not reap good returns for those good deeds you've done. But if you are not focused on some reciprocal effect, it would not matter if you were rewarded or not. With this in mind, detachment is an attitude to develop. When we reach out to others by offering our help, we can do so without the need for our name to be added to some list of contributors. Assist without expecting good returns. Also when considering the laws of cause and effect, if you contribute behaviors that cause someone to have a bad day, don't be surprised if your behavior boomerangs. It may not show up in the same form as you put it out there, but it is coming. Don't take a chance; treat people the way you want to be treated, plain and simple. For all you know, that someone you are kind to could be sitting on the other side of a table interviewing you for a most wanted job someday.

When we are having a great day, it's easy to be nice to others and to reach out a hand. But so often, when life throws us a big, fat, delicate water balloon disguised as a bag of money, we tend to turn around and treat others in ways they don't expect or deserve. As bosses, we fail to give employees a raise knowing they have more than earned it. We talk down to them; we may cause them to stand out in a crowd by loud-talking them, humiliating them in a meeting. Those of us who hold no such position in the work place may have, at some time, sabotaged our co-worker's efforts. And in so doing, we cause them to be reprimanded by the supervisor. We belittle their suggestions, or we tune them out. Some of us have jumped at the chance to point out the mistakes of others. We do this to make ourselves feel larger, more intelligent, and indispensable. We simply treat people with poor intentions all in effort to stroke our own ego. This type of (blind or otherwise) contribution to the collective consciousness is setting you up for failure. So think again, is it really worth it to mistreat others? You are already feeling miserable, why add more nails to the whipping stick?

Sometimes we focus on people we consider "mean" and wonder why they seem to have everything they want. And don't some of us become irate when we notice this around us? We can't understand why we work so hard to live an honest life only to suffer so much. Most of us know of someone whom we think is rotten to the core. This person appears to have everything anyone could ever want, the cars, the money, the jewelry, you name it. Let's say a man, for example, yells at the mail carrier and honks his horn at a frail, old lady pushing her walker across his driveway. And if that's not enough, he leaves his dog out overnight in frigid weather barking to be let inside. "How come he has it so good and I don't? I'm the one who prays and gives until it hurts. Why do mean people have it so much better than I?" In the past, I have asked these questions myself.

Today, I have realized such a person has done good deeds in the past, possibly serving others. As he performed in a life supportive way back then, his behavior resulted in earning brownie points in heaven, so to speak. So in this lifetime, the man you call "mean" is reaping the benefit of those past actions. At some point, he will run out of the brownie points and begin to reap the results of negative behavior performed in the present life. Some of us may secretly wish to be around to see this person fall when they run out of good merits. Okay, I was guilty of this one too in the past, but this type of thinking is not helpful, as it again contributes to the collective problems of the world. And because it is unproductive to think in this way, there are consequences.

Better yet, it's best to focus on you. How are you impacting the world with your thoughts and behavior?

Are you acting in a mean way or have you already begun making improvements on how you think? Whatever fascinates you grows on you. In other words, when we place our attention on another person's faults or differences, we start to present those same qualities. How often have you been around someone who speaks with an accent that you have picked up without intending? As the person speaks, we are deeply in the crux of how the words we hear are pronounced so differently than how we ourselves talk. When we listen, we notice the unique way emphases are placed on syllables, the tone of voice or how certain letters are pronounced. We give such attention to the way this person speaks that it becomes a part of us. Over time, we develop somewhat of an accent ourselves. Therefore, the next time you point out behavior in others, notice how much of that behavior is also a part of you. But of equal importance, think about what causes a person to act mean spirited. Chances are, such an individual has been badly hurt along the way and decided to shut down to others.

Behavior Disguised as Help

Now, about gossip: "He said, she said" has never really turned out a good story. Someone always messes up the plot to the point that the characters end up getting hurt. The habit of gossiping is malicious and never has any good intent, yet people do it. This is because gossipers have a negative self-image. They create falsehoods about another person to appear to be superior and in the know. In addition, those who spread gossip sometimes try to pretend they only want to help someone.

The idea is "If they knew how bad they... [looked, walked, talked or smelled, for example] they will want to change so I'm just helping them to see the error of their ways. Don't shoot the messenger." The "I know" syndrome has such a person thinking she has the right to point out another person's faults, weaknesses, or way of being in the world. They deem others as unacceptable while verbally attacking them; they think they can fix the problem they see in someone else. What they don't seem to know is the unpleasantness they spot in others is a reflection of what is within them.

How many times have you bought something and suddenly it seems as if everyone has it? When I was 19 years old, I bought a Volkswagen Beetle. As soon as I drove off of the car dealer's lot, I saw Beetles everywhere. The reason there seemed to be so many all of a sudden is because the moment I bought the car, I instantly familiarized my consciousness with the small vehicle; it had become a part of my awareness. Every car I saw that looked like mine suddenly stood out from all the other cars. It's like the prom dress in high school; a teenaged girl wants the unique one no one else will have. Then, when the young woman shows up at the dance, she finds others wearing not only the same dress she bought but in fact, some girls have the same color as the one she chose. In other words, if you have never seen a yellow-belly sap sucker, you certainly cannot point one out now can you? What we see in others is a mirror image of how we present ourselves; it shows up to help us work on our character defects.

You already know this material but your inability to fully understand is due to USB. No amount of what you know can fix anybody if it hasn't saved you from your own doom and gloom. Think about what else you can do instead of behaving in a familiar pattern. Acting differently than the way you are used to behaving can put you at the starting point of a new beginning. Once you get better at listening to others tell you how to stop the madness that is your life, you can begin to turn things around and relish the joy of living. For a change in your life, you might want to be the person who stops the gossip instead of starting or spreading it. Imagine how that would feel?

Mean People Don't Really Suck

I lived with my grandmother and because of the experiences I endured while residing under her roof, I walked around with a frown on my face. As my mother described it, my bottom lip was "poked out" all the time. The first time my grandparents allowed my mother to visit my siblings and me, she looked at me with her arms stretched out and said, "Awe, come here baby." Without returning the gesture, I replied instead with, "Name ain't baby, name Squatty" which was my nick name as a child. Over time, I would enjoy my mother's company and would hug her neck in the way small children show affection. Now that I'm an adult, I understand I was acting mean due to the abuse that had been projected toward me while living in that house. But no matter what, my mother showered me with her love and affection. She would pick up my tiny frame and kiss me on my cheek wearing her red lipstick. And when I didn't respond in kind during her very rare visits, she would continue to hold me on her lap while she visited with the others, bouncing me and caressing me lovingly. She didn't return my behavior with an attitude of, "Well screw you then!"

It's not at all easy to offer compassion when you feel mistreated by someone. But there are many ways to respond without returning the hate. When people act like a bear, offer love and patience instead. You can just acknowledge with a kind glance while saying nothing in response. You can verbalize some understanding words or just walk away. When we react to negative people with like attitudes, we have no need to be alarmed when we get unfavorable responses. It is in math where two negatives equal a positive; in other words, two wrong actions don't make a right one. When treated badly, turn the other cheek; change your mind, that is, your thoughts, about the person you think is hurting you. Respond with patience and you'll find you will come out on top. Think about when you are what you call "being mean"; it is at that very moment when you would appreciate love, patience, and understanding, not a mirror image of unkindness.

Sometimes when you consciously set out to hurt others for some perceived wrong done to you, your karma may come back instantly. In this case, you won't have to die and wait for another human body. Misbehave and you might notice the effect coming back to you sooner than you expect. Now, as you make life supportive thought choices, you may find your good bouncing back to you just as fast. Your good karma may appear in this present life and maybe in the same day. Here's another tip: The next time you feel agitated as a result of some negative gesture or remark directed at you, be conscious enough to step outside of that feeling. Forget what you need and consider the needs of the person in front of you. When you meet wretchedness with love, you will notice the sudden feeling of your own mood shifting as your own darkness dissolves.

Chapter XI

Boredom

*"Enlightenment isn't served at
a drive-through window."*

There are those of you who have all the tools in your lap for eradicating your problems but you simply won't lift a finger to use them. You complain, "Oh that book, it's boring so I put it down," or "Oh yeah, my mantra... I don't have the time to meditate." You have met holy people, you may even have an altar in some tiny area of your home, yet you refuse to actually take the next step. You seem to want quick fixes; drive through enlightenment in the way you get a box of fries at a fast food window. You want something that will keep you from having to put too much effort into being happy.

This group might abuse alcohol and/or other drugs to cope with their boredom. They hold down jobs and to some extent have lasting relationships, yet they are not able to figure out why they are not progressing. They simply feel stuck. These people behave as if they want someone to do it for them, to be spoon fed heaven on earth.

It's as if they don't want to be inconvenienced. From watching others around them, they know an inner journey is time consuming and at times seems intense so they avoid a path that could possibly set them free. A quiet voice inside may beckon them to go to church, for example, but they ignore it at all cost. They don't want to take the time to do an inner search. It's always a good idea to them but they just "don't have the time." They will support your journey, give you rides to the ashram, or encourage you to go to church when you don't feel like it. They may go out of their way to accompany you to religious events, but only once or twice.

Those who struggle in this way may also have anxiety or may be depressed as they sleep long hours, watch a lot of TV, or over-eat. They tend to be procrastinators, putting things off for the future while wondering why they have not accomplished everything they have planned. People in this category may start a task and give up somewhere in the middle, thinking it was a wrong choice to start it. They can be really good at helping others solve their problems and have a kind heart and usually don't participate in negative behaviors against others.

If this describes you, I suggest you see a therapist to help you figure out what is most important to you. Take some time to address those issues regarding a spiritual path if that interests you. If you are curious about spirituality, find an unbiased adviser, someone who can offer many views on matters around God and spirituality without proselytizing their own agenda. Make sure the person also practices some inner form of awareness and has many years of experience helping others in this area.

Hire a life coach to help you plan out your future and assist you in staying on task. Once you gain some clarity, you will find you have the time to journey inward. Right now, you have so much inner turmoil or confusion; you can't clearly navigate your outer world. What you see going on in your life is only a reflection of what is going on in your head. Take the time and get some other perspective on your concerns; you don't have to do it alone.

Final Notes

*"Admit your weaknesses, face
your challenges and get back
in the running of your life."*

f you have read this far, it means you are one who is making great strides on your quest for happiness; you haven't given up. No doubt you will find your way and become successful in your journey forward; it's inevitable. As you keep up the search with wholeheartedness, you will find you are chipping away all that isn't your true nature. Sometimes we have to throw our hands in the air and give up as we may try too hard to get it. We can't see what is often in front of us; we dismiss a clue because it seems too simple or we don't approve of the source. Take a look in the mirror. I want you to get that you are the only one who holds the handle of your life.

Get it because you no longer want to suck people up into your drama. Get it because you are sick and tired of friends leaving you for dead. And, if you have children, you do not want to unconsciously teach them how to suffer because it's not what you say to them, but how you live your life that they notice. Our children tend to practice what we do until they master it. Do your best to teach them how to be happy through modeling a different way of being. And if they have already seen you bottom out, here is a wonderful opportunity to show them how to stand up tall again. Show them how to admit your weaknesses, to face your challenges and get back in the running for your life. You're good for it, and someday, they will tell you why they are so proud of you.

You no longer have to miss out on the glory of God that is YOU. You say you are a lawyer or a salesman, for example, because that is what you do (for a living). Well, a living God dwells inside of you because that is what God does. So, it goes without saying, God is you. You are God.

I want you to understand the part only YOU can play in how to manage your life. I want you to get that your life is only in Your hands. Now is the time to handle it differently; be the change you want to see in your life. Show up in the next moment with new thoughts on, in the way you may have shown up in new clothes on the first day of school as a child. Have the resolve to persevere, have the gumption to be happy, have the courage to hear the truth and change how you think. Hold on to your dream of freedom -- a life without suffering. The great leader Mahatma Gandhi said our thoughts become words, our words become our actions, and because of this, we have to keep our intentions positive.

Addictions

As for addictions, they can be hard to break and being hooked on negative thinking is no different. I have heard it said, those with food obsessions, for example, struggle exceptionally hard because they have to eat. The argument states: Their source of addiction is ever present as the physical body depends on food for survival. "So they can't get away from that which is the basis of their addictions," some may say. But when you stop and think about it, it is not the food that is the problem. Those with food issues have to practice a different attitude about it to help them overcome their struggle with it. And many are quite successful and go on to live fulfilling lives.

Like food addicts, you can change your attitudes both about life and how it unfolds for you. Because you now understand from a deeper level that you hold the only key to your happiness, you can give up negative thinking. Start now to create a rewarding existence filled with supportive friends and family. Why not create wealth? It can be done and you are just the person to do it. For all you know, enlightenment may be your experience with the next breath you take.

More About The Author

Teral E. Champion was born in Washington, D.C. She earned a Bachelor of Science degree in Psychology from Edgewood College located in Madison, Wisconsin. At age 50, she received a Master's of Social Work degree at the University of Wisconsin-Milwaukee. Currently, Teral holds a professional license in social work in the state of Iowa. In Wisconsin, Teral was licensed as a special education assistant after completing her training with the Madison Metropolitan school District.

During her graduate studies, Teral has practiced as a student therapist at the Zeblocki Medical Center for veterans in Milwaukee, Wisconsin and has practiced as a therapist at the Ottumwa Psychiatric Clinic in Ottumwa, Iowa. She has provided case management at the Salvation Army in Madison, Wisconsin, organized and facilitated workshops on insomnia, led empowerment groups for women and created fun activities for teen girls. In addition, Teral has held the position of acting clinic administrator for the Family Center, a mental health clinic in Madison, Wisconsin.

Just after high school, Teral learned Transcendental Meditation ™ and has been practicing this technique for over 30 years. In 1980, she later moved her family of two to the small Midwestern town of Fairfield, Iowa, where she attended Maharishi International University. There at the institution, she learned advanced methods of TM.

Currently, Teral is working on completing a book relating to a simple practice she created for visualizing peace. She is also in the process of creating a retail website where much of the proceeds from sales will go to help homeless women and their families. She is also looking forward to assisting spiritual groups in this way. You will soon be able to view her online store at www.sillymonktees.com. There, you will find unique T-shirts and other items that speak to the journey of spiritual seekers in a comedic tone.

In her spare time, Teral loves creating art with various media and also enjoys writing poetry. She has an interest in music, and in science, she holds a fascination with the cosmos. Other interests include watching sunsets, spending time in nature and enjoying the company of animals.

References

Luke 6:31 (New International Version).